A VISIT TO

Poland

Vic Parker

www.heinemann.co.uk/library
Visit our website to find out more information about Heinemann Library books.

To order:
 Phone 44 (0) 1865 888066
 Send a fax to 44 (0) 1865 314091
Visit the Heinemann Bookshop at www.heinemann.co.uk/library to browse our catalogue and order online.

First published in Great Britain by Heinemann Library, Halley Court, Jordan Hill, Oxford OX2 8EJ, part of Pearson Education. Heinemann is a registered trademark of Pearson Education Ltd.

Editorial: Diyan Leake
Design: Joanna Hinton-Malivoire and Philippa Jenkins
Picture research: Mica Brancic
Production: Duncan Gilbert

Originated by Modern Age
Printed and bound in China by South China Printing Co. Ltd

ISBN 978 0 431 087375 (hardback)
12 11 10 09 08
10 9 8 7 6 5 4 3 2 1

ISBN 978 0 431 087511 (paperback)
12 11 10 09 08
10 9 8 7 6 5 4 3 2 1

British Library Cataloguing in Publication Data
Parker, Victoria
 A visit to Poland
 1. Poland – Social conditions – 1980 –
 – Juvenile literature
 2. Poland – Geography – Juvenile literature
 3. Poland – Social life and customs – 21st
 century   – Juvenile literature
I. Title II. Poland
943.8'057

Acknowledgements
The publishers would like to thank the following for permission to reproduce photographs: © Alamy pp. **7** (tompiodesign.com), **10** (Gavin Hellier), **11** (Philip Wolmuth), **12** (Simon Reddy), **13** (Steve Skjold), **14** (Caro/Bastian), **15** (Frances Roberts), **16** (Caro), **18** (Caro), **19** (Konrad Zelazowski), **20** (Rob Brimson), **22** (Pegaz), **23** (Jenny Matthews), **25** (John Cairns (Poland)), **26** (Andrzej Gorzkowski), **27** (Jim West); © Corbis pp. **5** (Rudy Sulgan), **28** (The Art Archive/Alfredo Dagli Orti); © Getty Images pp. **17** (Piotr Malecki), **24** (Stone/Frank Herholdt); © Photolibrary pp. **6** (Arcangel Images/Piotr Ciesla), **8** (voller Ernst/Roland Marske), **9** (Mauritius/Mattes Mattes), **29** (Mauritius/Henryk Thomasz Kaiser); © Rex Features p. **21** (Eric Vidal).

Cover photograph reproduced with permission of © Getty Images (Robert Harding World Imagery).

Our thanks to Nick Lapthorn for his comments in the preparation of this book.

Every effort has been made to contact copyright holders of any material reproduced in this book. Any omissions will be rectified in subsequent printings if notice is given to the publishers.

Contents

Any words appearing in bold, **like this**, are explained in the Glossary.

Poland

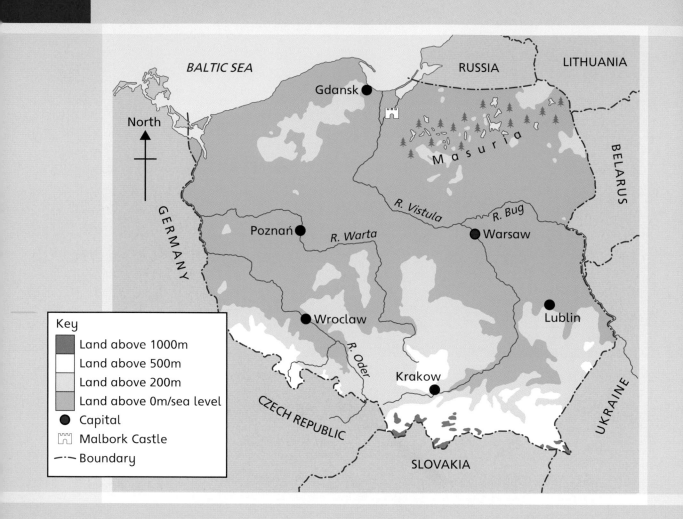

Key
- Land above 1000m
- Land above 500m
- Land above 200m
- Land above 0m/sea level
- ● Capital
- Malbork Castle
- – · – Boundary

BALTIC SEA · RUSSIA · LITHUANIA · Gdansk · North · M a s u r i a · BELARUS · R. Vistula · R. Bug · GERMANY · Poznań · R. Warta · Warsaw · Wroclaw · Lublin · R. Oder · Krakow · UKRAINE · CZECH REPUBLIC · SLOVAKIA

Poland is a big country. It is in Europe. The Baltic Sea is to the north of it. Poland is **surrounded by** many countries.

4

Some cities in Poland are more than 800 years old. There are many interesting old streets as well as lots of exciting modern buildings.

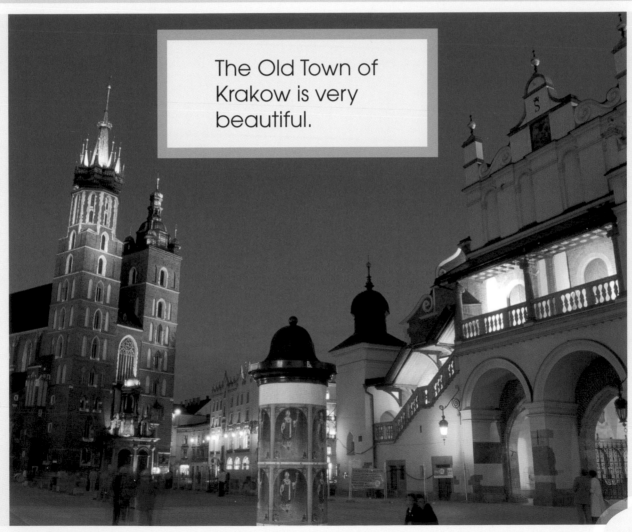

The Old Town of Krakow is very beautiful.

Land

Much of Poland is farmland.

There are forests and lakes in north-east Poland. The centre of the country is flat and low with wide rivers. It is easy to grow crops there.

In the south of Poland there are mountain ranges. There are wild animals in the mountains. These include **bison**, bears, **lynx**, wildcats, wolves, and golden eagles.

Landmarks

The area of Masuria has thousands of lakes. People go there to enjoy water sports such as sailing and canoeing.

Masuria is a favourite holiday place.

8

Malbork Castle was built 700 years ago.

Malbork Castle is one of the world's largest brick castles. It is three castles in one. Inside the outer walls lies a smaller castle. Inside that there is an even smaller castle, on a hill.

Homes

Polish houses on the outskirts of cities often have three floors.

Most people in Poland live in large cities. In the city centres, many people live in apartments. On the **outskirts** there is more space, so people like to build big, modern houses.

There are many small, older houses made of wood in the countryside. People from the cities often own them as holiday homes.

Country homes are usually much simpler than city homes.

Food

Favourite foods in Poland are bread, sausages, fish, beetroot, cabbage, potatoes and cake. Poles like strong, hot, sour, or sweet flavours.

A normal *obiad* is soup, a main course, and dessert.

In Poland, the main meal is called *obiad*. It is eaten when children come home from school in the afternoon. After *obiad*, supper is at about 8 or 9 in the evening.

Clothes

Polish people wear modern clothes, like jeans and trainers. In winter, they have to wrap up warm because it gets very cold.

Young people enjoy wearing fashionable clothes.

People sometimes wear **traditional** Polish **costume** for weddings and festivals. The clothes are brightly coloured and decorated with **embroidery** and ribbons.

Work

Many people in Poland work in service industries. This means that they work in places such as schools, hospitals, sports centres, train stations, offices and shops.

Many Polish people are skilled electricians, plumbers, and builders.

Other Poles have jobs in factories, in mines, and on building sites. Some Polish people work on farms, raising animals and growing crops for food.

Transport

Roads in Poland often get jammed with cars and lorries, because there are not many motorways. Many cities have a tram system, to help people travel about easily.

A tram is a type of bus that runs on rails.

Warsaw's underground train system is called the Metro.

Poland has an excellent railway network – including a high-speed railway line. This links the **capital** city, Warsaw, with other important cities. Warsaw has an underground railway line, too.

Language

In Poland, people speak Polish. Polish has a similar alphabet to English, but the letters Q, V, and X are not used in Polish words.

Polish uses **accents** to make some letters sound different.

Children have to start learning a foreign language from the age of 7.

Many Poles can speak, read, and write English as well as Polish. Most Polish children learn English in school. Some children also learn German.

School

Polish children start school when they are 7 and leave when they are 18. They study maths, history, geography, science, art, languages, music, and physical education.

Polish pupils do not wear school uniform.

Polish pupils have to buy all their own books and writing equipment.

The school day begins at 8 in the morning and finishes at lunchtime. Many children do activities in the afternoons such as extra music or sports lessons.

Free time

Many Polish people enjoy cycling in their free time.

Polish people love spending time with their family and friends, chatting over a meal or watching TV. They also enjoy outdoor activities such as dog-walking and cycling.

In winter, many Polish people head for the mountains at weekends. There are sports centres there where you can go skiing, snowboarding, and ice skating.

Some Polish mountains are covered in snow from November to March.

Celebrations

Christmas is the biggest celebration of the year in Poland. People have a special meal on Christmas Eve. Then they sing carols and go to church at midnight.

A name day may be celebrated like a birthday.

Many Polish people are named after Christian **saints** or other people from the past. They may celebrate the saint's special day as their "name day".

The Arts

Fryderyk Chopin was born in Poland. He was one of the greatest composers who ever lived. He wrote beautiful piano music, taking his ideas from Polish **folk tunes**.

Chopin lived from 1810 to 1849.

Wycinanki is used to decorate some **traditional** houses.

The Polish art of paper cutting is called *wycinanki* (pronounced vee-chee-non-kee). People fold and cut layers of coloured paper into bright designs.

Factfile

Name   The full name of Poland is the Republic of Poland.

Capital   The **capital** is Warsaw.

Language The main language is Polish. Many people also speak English and German.

Population There are about 38.5 million people living in Poland.

Money   Polish money is called the złoty (pronounced zwotih).

Religions Most Poles are Roman Catholic, which is a type of Christianity.

Products Poland produces clothes, glass, china, electrical goods, cars, buses, helicopters, planes, ships, medicines, chemicals, and food products.

Words you can learn

dzień dobry (JEYN dobry)	hello
proszę (proh-sheng)	please
dziękuję (jenKOO-yeng)	thank you
tak (tahk)/nie (nyeh)	yes/no
do widzenia (doh vit-SENyah)	goodbye
jeden (YEH-den)	one
dwa (dvah)	two
trzy (tzhih)	three

Glossary

accent mark above or below a letter to show you how to pronounce it

bison a large, wild animal, similar to a cow, with long, shaggy hair

capital the city where the government is based

costume a set of clothes worn by people in a certain place or certain time in history

embroidery coloured thread that is stitched in patterns or pictures onto cloth or clothing

folk tunes music that has been popular for a long time with people who live in a certain area or country

lynx a wild animal of the cat family. It has brown hair, sometimes with dark spots on it, pointed ears, and a short tail.

outskirts the areas on the edge of a town or city

saint a person who lived in a very good and holy way

surrounded by has around it on all sides

traditional the way things have been done or made for a long time

Index